20 WAYS
TO DRAW
A MUSTACHE

AND 23 OTHER
FUNNY FACES AND FEATURES

CARA BEAN

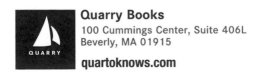

A Book for Artists, Designers, and Doodlers

Quarry Books
100 Cummings Center, Suite 406L
Beverly, MA 01915
quartoknows.com

This library edition published in 2016 by Walter Foster Publishing,
a division of Quarto Publishing Group USA Inc.
6 Orchard Road, Suite 100
Lake Forest, CA 92630

Distributed in the United States and Canada by
Lerner Publisher Services
241 First Avenue North
Minneapolis, MN 55401 U.S.A.
www.lernerbooks.com

First Library Edition

Library of Congress Cataloging-in-Publication Data

Bean, Cara, author.
  20 ways to draw a mustache and 23 other funny faces and features : a book for artists, designers, and doodlers / Cara Bean. -- First Library Edition.
      pages cm
  "First published in the United States of America in 2014 by Quarry Books, a member of Quarto Publishing Group USA Inc."
  ISBN 978-1-942875-00-0
1. Face in art. 2. Notebooks. I. Title. II. Title: Twenty ways to draw a mustache and 23 other funny faces and features.
  NC770.B29 2015
  743.4'9--dc23
                                                                                                    2015031368

9 8 7 6 5 4 3 2 1

CONTENTS

INTRODUCTION

20 Ways to Draw a Mustache is a fun and interactive book designed to help you explore a wide variety of approaches to drawing. It encourages experimentation with media and explores different ways of imagining and seeing. Inside you'll find plenty of examples to delight and inspire.

bean characters: waterproof ink, colored pencil, and watercolor

Human features, limbs, expressions, actions, and character types can be unlimited resources for drawing inspiration. There are countless ways to depict human qualities with creativity and playfulness. In this book you'll find twenty-four themes drawn in a variety of styles. For each theme, the subject matter or shape remains the same, but the approach to drawing it differs. You will see twenty ways to draw each topic: Perhaps you can come up with twenty more?

Drawing doesn't have to be stressful or require lofty expectations. You may discover that simply drawing a theme twenty times will lead to surprising revelations. Keep in mind that mistakes are a welcome part of the process. Drawing is best when you can relax, grab your favorite pens and pencils, and just let the doodling happen. Observe what can occur when you remain open to experimentation and allow your imagination to wander. Just follow along with where your pencil would like to travel on the page. You can explore the possibilities of a shape, investigate different line qualities, and invent various ways to create textures. You will discover that the more often you draw, the more confidence you will build.

There is a great degree of freedom in how you may approach subject matter that interests you. People watching can be a fascinating endeavor for artists. We can simply place ourselves in a public space and draw the many hair shapes, colors, and textures that cross our path.

HOW TO USE THIS BOOK

There are twenty drawings for each theme shown. Some are very simple; some, more complex. Some are realistic while others are reduced to their most basic elements. Some are rendered accurately; others ignore scale and proportion. Look at the images and select those that interest you. What is it about them that pulls you in? Can you draw something similar? Find new ways to reconfigure the shapes and lines that you see.

Maybe you can combine various features to invent new characters? Perhaps you will make monsters with twenty different kinds of eyes? Maybe try putting a mustache on a cat or a beard on a dog? Create a party where only people with mullets are invited!

Become comfortable with the idea that you can express yourself through drawing. Draw in a way that surprises and captivates your imagination. Explore different drawing tools and apply different techniques. Some drawings will work and others will be less successful. Enjoy the process and interpret your mistakes as potential creative possibilities. Enjoy the idea that we can draw a mustache in as many ways as there are mustaches in existence!

mustaches: waterproof ink and watercolor

Mustaches

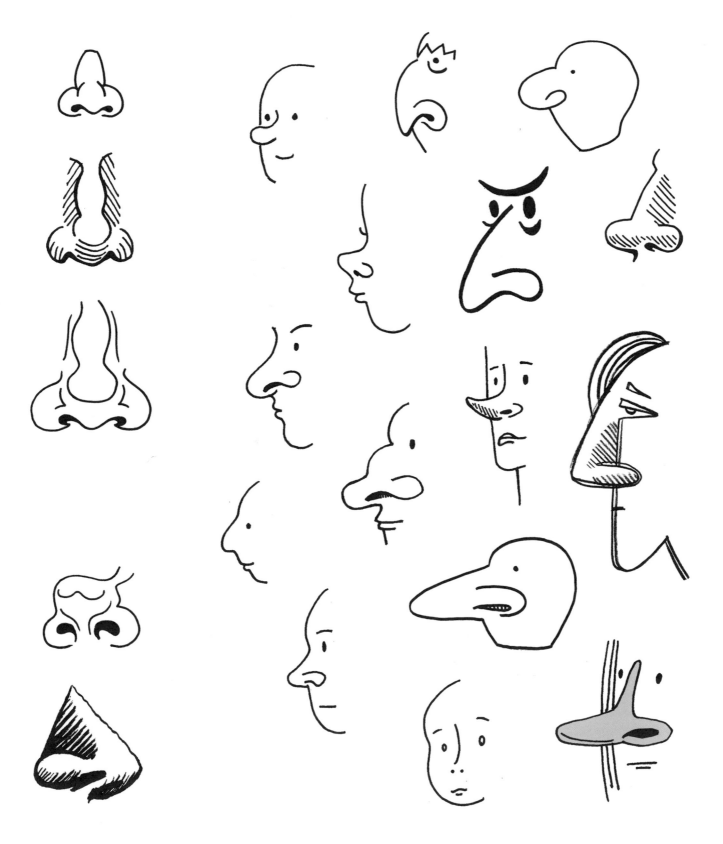

DRAW 20
Lips

EYES

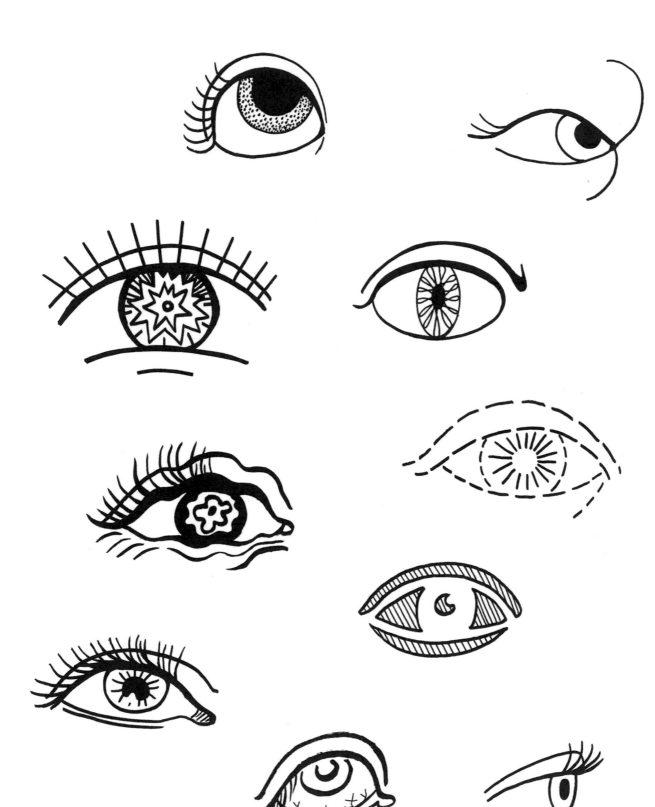

DRAW 20
Ears

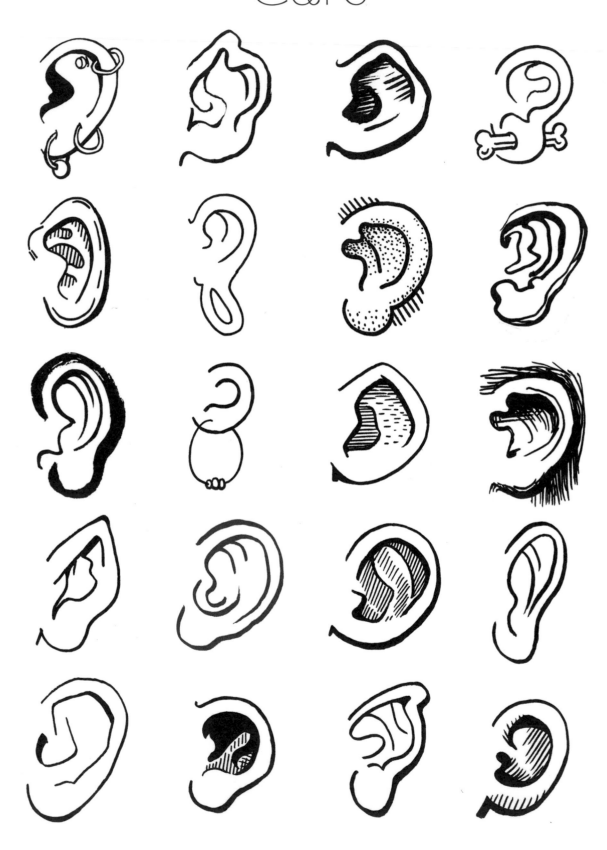

DRAW 20
Bean Characters

DRAW 20
STRAIGHT HAIRSTYLES

DRAW 20
CURLY HAIRSTYLES

Feet

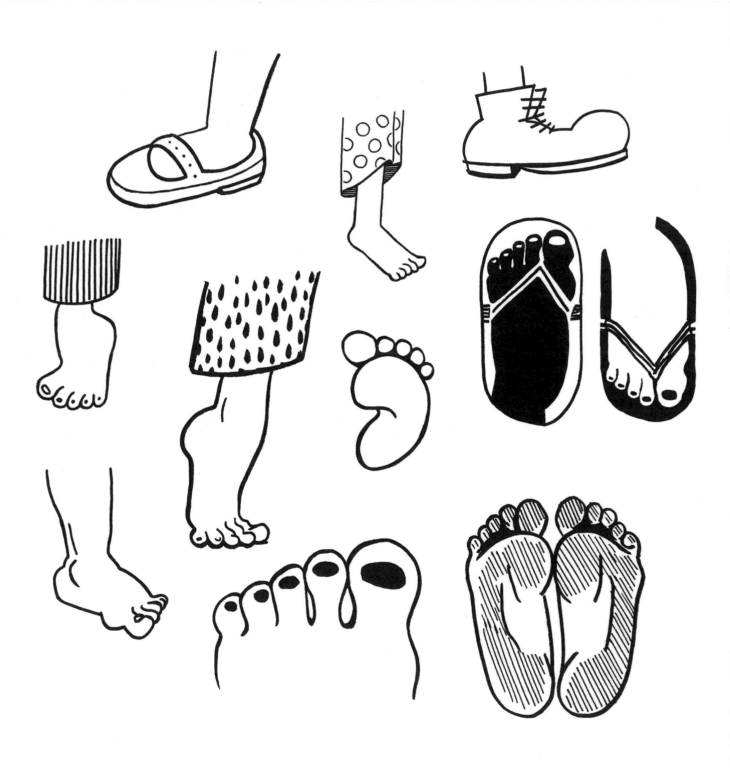

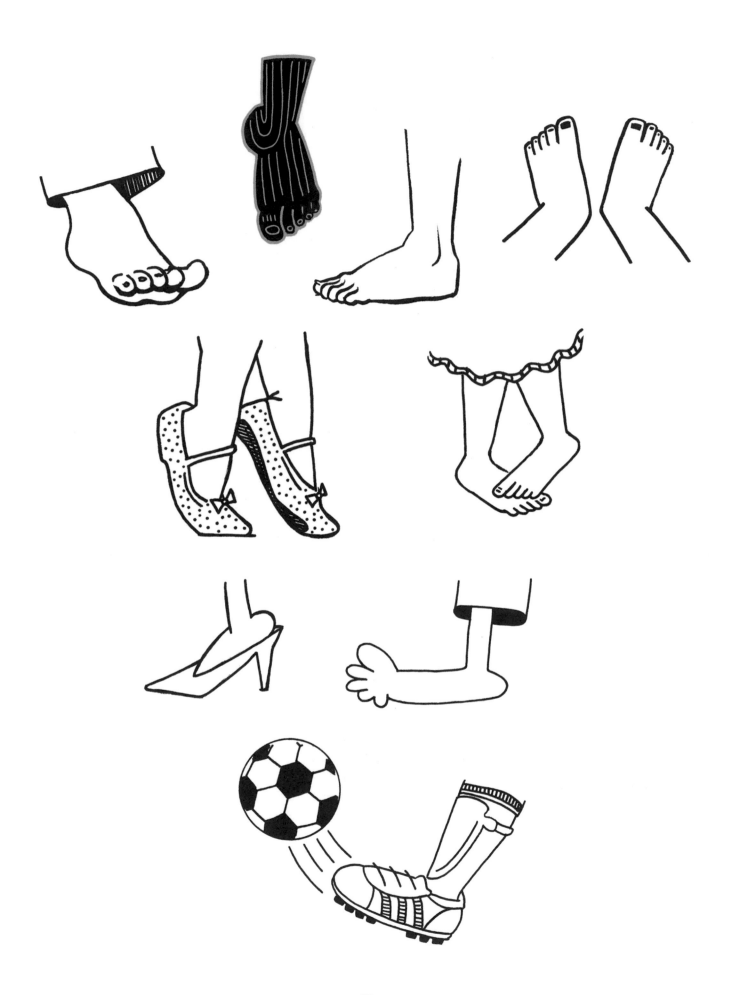

DRAW 20
Mullets

DRAW 20
Hands

Arms

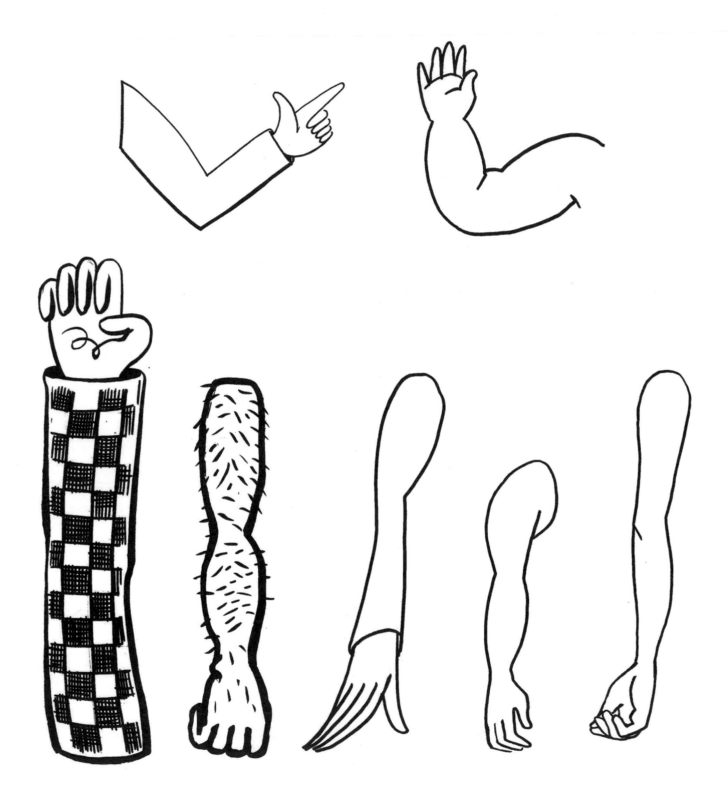

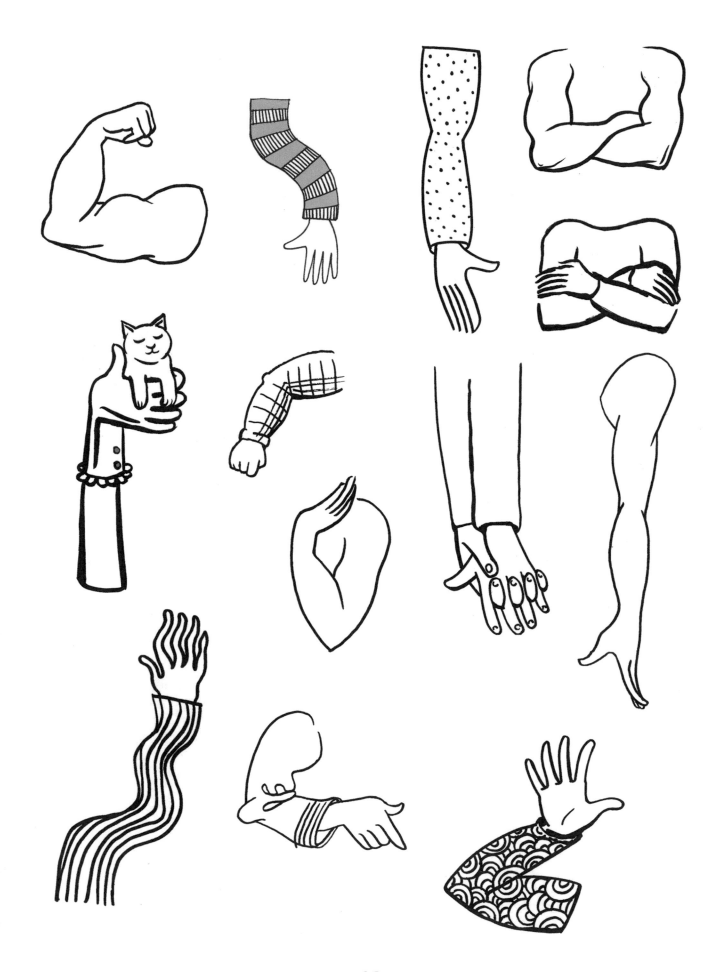

LEGS

FROWNS

DRAW 20
Emotions

DRAW 20
Braids

DRAW 20
CIRCLE CHARACTERS

DRAW 20
Walkers Walking

DRAW 20
EYEGLASSES

DRAW 20
EYEBROWS

DRAW 20
Different Ages

DRAW 20
Heart Characters

ABOUT THE ARTIST

Cara Bean is a cartoonist and art teacher from Concord, Massachusetts. She graduated with a master's degree in painting and drawing from the University of Washington, in Seattle. When she is not teaching, she makes comic books that relate to her life's experiences and fills sketchbooks with strange doodles. Cara likes: dogs, apes, tea, green hoodies, soup with crusty bread, people who walk alone and smile to themselves, hikes, mangos, befriending shy people, cats, libraries, thrift stores, Guadalajara, dancing with babies, crunchy leaves, owls, and nachos. Her students gather on Tuesdays after school for Illustration Club, which has become a place to draw and share ideas. Cara lives in a small cottage near Walden Pond with three wild dogs named Howie, Jackie, and Jon. Learn more about Cara Bean at: badgigi.com, beandoodling.blogspot.com.